THERE IS NO DEATH, ONLY *Life*

MARIA VERDESCHI

ISBN: 978-1-7339340-0-8

Library of Congress Control Number: 2019905072

Printed in USA by Maria Verdeschi

The publisher has strived to be as accurate and complete as possible in the creation of this book.

This book is not intended for use as a source of health or medical advice. All readers are advised to seek services of competent professionals in health, medical, and related fields. Readers are cautioned to rely on their own judgment about their individual circumstances and to act accordingly.

The advice and strategies found within may not be suitable for every situation. This work is sold with the understanding that neither the author nor the publisher is held responsible for the results accrued from the advice in this book.

For more information, visit https://www.MariaVerdeschi.com/.

For bulk book orders, contact Maria@MariaVerdeschi.com.

Michael, Grace, Maria, and Anne Marie

This book is dedicated to my children, Michael, Anne Marie, and Grace, who have unquestionably supported my gifts and journey.

This book is also dedicated to my mom for being my greatest guide from the other side and inspiring my deadline with her April birth date.

This book would not have been possible without my clients who were courageous enough to come forward and share their life stories. I'm honored to have had the opportunity to know all of you and share in your spiritual growth and healing.

Lastly, I dedicate this book to everyone who has died in fear. I'm spreading the news that there is no death, only life, so others can cross over peacefully.

Table of Contents

Foreword

A psychic medium has a tough job. We are expected to show compassion to others, but are often misunderstood. We are expected to be 100% accurate, but are human. We are healers of grief, but often grieving ourselves. We must be objective in our readings, but constantly trying to understand the subjective psychic information we regularly receive. As psychics and mediums, we constantly deal with understanding and coming to terms with our unique and complex life.

In Maria's book, she shares client stories, as well as her own personal history of coming in touch with her own gifts. By sharing her own path as a psychic and medium, she illustrates the way we can all become in touch with our own inner healing and psychic gifts. She also shares personal stories of clients who were moved by evidential readings--readings that were helpful, healing and moving, but also contained specific information which could only be obtained by speaking with the client's loved ones.

A reading has so much healing potential. It allows the loved ones to express deep inner thoughts, it allows the client to move on, and it allows the medium to be a vessel of healing. Maria's client stories help any reader to understand the true healing power of mediumship.

I met Maria a couple of years ago when I was teaching a course on mediumship. Immediately, I noticed that Maria had a wonderful way of framing evidential information with healing information when she was doing a reading for someone. For example, in one reading, I recall her bringing through the word blueberries connected to a Grandmother in Spirit. The student she was reading later revealed her grandmother had a love of blueberries and had blueberry bushes.

I have recommended Maria to many clients and friends to receive readings, and I have no doubt that Maria has a pure connection to Spirit. I would have to say out of the hundreds of students I have had, Maria is probably one of the most gifted I have mentored. She receives very evidential information from departed loved ones.

For the last 10 years, I have devoted my life to serving Spirit, helping people connect with their intuition, and helping them connect with the Other Side. One of the great gifts I have had in teaching about the Spirit world is to mentor students who have a true capacity to hear, feel, and see Spirit, and are able to give brilliant messages from loved ones. I am honored to be a part of Maria's journey as a psychic medium.

Enjoy the book, and welcome!

Thomas John, Medium and Psychic, Author of **Never Argue with a Dead Person: True and Unbelievable Stories from the Other Side.**

Acknowledgments

Special thanks to all the people who assisted me with this book. I'd especially like to thank Lisbeth Tanz for her editing and seeing my vision; Diana M. Needham for her expert guidance with publishing and launching the book; Jody Mitchell for technical writing assistance (plus support and encouragement to keep me on course); Jim Aho for photographic editing and flexibility; and Michelle Barr for getting things in place.

I also want to acknowledge Georgia Lambert, my spiritual teacher, who always had the answers when I needed them. She possesses unlimited spiritual knowledge on all religions and beliefs and so much more.

Thank you from the bottom of my heart.

Chapter One

How It All Began

My story began at 248 Bread and Cheese Hollow Road in Northport, Long Island, New York. It was at this magical house where I discovered my abilities. My magical red house was located at the end of a long steep curved driveway near the top of a hill surrounded by trees and nature. I loved to pretend I was riding a horse when I climbed the big rock in the front yard. At the bottom of the driveway, my father made a sign with the perfect description, "Storybook Hill."

Our neighbors at the bottom of the hill had a horse. I loved visiting that horse and having conversations with him. It was always a highlight of my day. One day, the horse got out and, instead of running toward the bottom of the hill, it ran toward the top of the hill to visit us. He was so beautiful and magnificent.

We shared our driveway with the neighbors above us. If you continued past our house, you'd arrive at Clive Hendrick's house at the top of the hill. Clive was my best friend, and we must have run up and down the dirt path that connected our yards a million times! Clive's house was also magical to me because it was surrounded by trees too. While our home sat on two acres, the Hendrick's property sat on six and included a much loved inground pool, which was adjacent to the large pool house. Clive's mother, Irma, who spoke with a heavy German accent, tended to fascinating and amazing plants in the greenhouse attached to their home.

I loved playing at Clive's house and watching *Mister Rogers' Neighborhood*, *The Jack LaLanne Show* where he'd demonstrate exercises, and *The Joy of Painting* with Bob Ross teaching viewers how to paint. My favorite shows to watch there were *H.R. Pufnstuf* and *Kimba the White Lion*. Later in life, I had the opportunity to meet Jean, the artist who made the head of Pufnstuf. I believe it wasn't a coincidence that we met. I'm still blessed for having her in my life. Television was an outlet for me. I loved the shows that made me happy because they allowed me to forget—for a while—the troubles my mother was experiencing at the time.

I've also always been hypersensitive to the energy around me and aware of how others feel. This ability goes all the way back to when I was in my crib. I discovered that I could sense energy from future events, like when something bad was about to happen. A four-year-old really doesn't think too much about such things. It's no surprise that I do a lot of energy work and healing in my life today; I've been doing it since the day I was born!

My grandma called me the smiling baby because she said I always woke up smiling. I constantly worried about people; I wanted to make sure they were happy. If they were sad, I would do what was in my power to put a smile on their face. I'm the youngest of four and have always been different from them. I suppose you could say I'm the Pollyanna of the group. I can always find the positive in everything; I consciously choose to see the good side of situations rather than the bad.

My Room

My bedroom in our house was small and painted a light shade of pink. I remember being in my crib, which was against the same wall as the window. I started getting messages in that crib, and I can remember standing up and listening to the spirits. When I moved into my "big girl" twin bed, it was placed on a different wall. Other furniture included a bookshelf painted the same pink color as walls and a tall dresser next to the door to the hallway. I loved the lamp on my dresser because it had a nightlight in the shape of a birdhouse on it. I depended on my nightlight. I remember awakening one night to find the bulb had burned out. I was terrified of the darkness! My room also included a closet with a brown sliding door, which was always closed. It may sound cliché, but I can still feel the negative energy emanating from behind that closet door.

My room seemed like a hub of conversation. Twice I crossed the hall to my parents' room to tell them there were people in my room. After being told the second time that no one was in my room, I understood that I was different. I never mentioned anything about the people in my room to them or anyone else for that matter.

Bedtime was always scary. That was when everyone in my room wanted to be heard and get their message to me. Despite what my parents thought, it was pretty loud in my room. I was so afraid of bedtime that I used to run from the door, jump into bed, and pull the covers over my head to feel safe. I'd politely ask them to quiet down, and they usually would. Because I had a bit of an understanding with them, I'd also remind them that it wasn't nice to scare me. And I had no idea why the messages would come to me or what to do with them. I slept with my stuffed brown dog with floppy ears that my grandmother had given to me when I was four for protection.

It's said that the separation between us and the beyond loosens as we fall asleep. I believe this, for as a child I'd hear sounds while half asleep, like someone was knocking on the bedroom door. To this day, at times I'll hear soft knocking sounds or someone walking in my room as I'm poised between wakefulness and sleep. Of course, when I fully wake up, no one is there.

Outside

The voices weren't relegated only to the nighttime. I remember an experience that still makes me laugh. I was playing by myself in the backyard on a hot and sunny day. Out of nowhere, I heard, "You are here to help others. You will be working with a group."

Now your average four-year-old would run inside and tell an adult what she heard. Not me. I automatically answered, "Okay," and kept playing. I treated it as if it were a normal everyday occurrence—because for me it was.

Being outside was truly magical for me, and I wasn't afraid to be alone on our two acres. I was lost in my own happy world. The outside energy was safe and nurturing. Everything was so alive: the trees, plants, insects, and birds. I felt nature at a high vibration. Everything was living and breathing and speaking! The land had a lot of history, which explains all the arrowheads my siblings and I found. The land had a story that wanted to be told.

As I played, spirits would join me for conversations. Well, they weren't really conversations like you might have—no one was talking aloud. These talks were in "thought form" in my head. At the time, I believed the conversations were *my* thoughts, even though my intuition said otherwise. During these conversations, I'd sometimes "see" things in what I can best describe as like a dream state. I'd also often feel the spirit's emotions. It's like when you recall a memory, and then pictures start to form in your head. As this is happening, you might remember a conversation that went along with the memories and pictures as well as the feelings you had at the time.

Michigan

We moved from our magical house on Long Island to a Detroit, Michigan, suburb when I was eight. It was a painful move for my entire family, especially my mother, who fell into a depression for two years. She tried to hide it from us, but I could "feel" it. Eventually, she went back to school to earn her master's degree in counseling. She became a well-known family counselor and truly helped a lot of people. Even after retirement, my mother remained close to some of her clients.

After we moved to Michigan, I couldn't hear spirits as clearly. I knew they were there, but they were quieter. In retrospect, I believe I chose to "turn down the volume" to make my life a little easier at the time. Moving away was hard enough, but managing this gift on top of that was too much. So, I chose to silence it and keep it my secret. It was easy to keep quiet about it because I just wanted to fit in. While that was my desire, fitting in was an illusion. I usually never felt like I belonged. What made me different kept me separate.

Over the years my abilities would peek out as if asking if I was ready for them yet. At age twenty-five,

I started listening just a little bit. I found it was like trying to listen to someone when the television or radio is blasting. I couldn't make out fully what they were saying, but I heard bits and pieces. At age forty, I allowed the door to open halfway, which allowed me to hear a little better. Fear was holding me back. I believed I wasn't ready for the messages or the changes that would happen if I opened the door completely. But I pushed past that fear. I've learned that fear serves no one; it only holds us back from what we need to do. I'm grateful for all my life lessons. Without them, I wouldn't have learned and grown. Through those lessons, my gifts have expanded. Today, I know that sharing my gifts is my reason for being.

Synchronicity has played a key role in my development. The teachers I needed to help me develop and learn to trust certain parts of my intuition have appeared in my life at the exact right moment, validating I'm on the right path. I've discovered that when life seems hard, it's because I've put obstacles in the way of my spiritual path progression. Taking ownership of the responsibility I have as the one who causes my own pain has been a deep, life-changing lesson for me.

By stepping out of my fear, I now own that my path is to help others get unstuck and lighten their emotional load. Death, losing a cherished loved one, and moving on from that event can be the most difficult experience for us to address. That's why the work I do is so very meaningful for my clients and me. These are the clear, overriding messages I share with everyone:

Your loved ones are always around you
and want to help.
Our loved ones don't want us to suffer.
They want life to be easier and for us to be happy.
And the most important message:

There is no death, only life.

As you read, you may find it helpful to take a moment to do the Relaxation Meditation I've created just for readers of this book. You can access it here: https://www.MariaVerdeschi.com/gift.

Chapter Two

THE READING PROCESS

Over the years, I've developed a process I use for every reading. Whether it's a phone reading or an in-person reading, my process begins when a reading is booked.

Honesty and Authenticity

I'm aware that what I do for a living is far beyond a "normal" job. I'm also aware that many people who advertise as psychic/mediums are, in the nicest of terms, charlatans. They prey on the emotions of grieving people. This makes me angry and sad. I live a truthful life as a psychic/medium every day. I don't pretend to be one; I am one.

I make a point of being transparent, honest, and authentic so I can be of the highest service to my clients. That's one reason I ask for almost no information up front. For example, I prefer to work only with a person's first name. If a client starts to tell me a story about their loved one, I stop them. I don't want to hear anything that might prejudice the reading.

Every client is treated with love and respect. My clients stay with me because they see and work with the real me. It's not an act or a show. I'm a grounded person living a drama-free life, and my priority is to stay emotionally and spiritually clear for my clients. Part of staying clear means abstaining from mind-altering substances such as alcohol. I live a quiet life to ensure my readings are the best they can be.

My Process

I begin the process by meditating. I bring my energy up to the higher level I use during readings. I sage beforehand to clear out negative energy and then light a candle as a sign that I'm ready. I know from experience that readings can be emotionally charged events for my clients. Fear is a common emotion because they're doing something unfamiliar that may be a little scary. I make sure to ease my clients' fears and concerns before we begin.

Once the reading begins, I don't try to rush the process. I encourage my clients to ask as many questions as they need to ask during our time together. As the reading progresses, I may ask my client questions. I'm only looking for a yes or no response, and, if the client starts giving more details, I will stop them.

As I listen, I write messages in my notebook. I'm frequently given information that no one knows except my client to validate who I'm connected with. Messages come through four of my five senses. I'll hear, see, feel, or smell their messages. They might show me things in the form of a movie or pull out the family photo album for me to see. Sometimes I can smell smoke if they were a smoker or smell the scent of heavy perfume. Their mannerisms from life come out in readings. I'll feel their energy come in and feel the emotions of their death, their life, and the love they have for the one receiving the message.

If I don't understand the message I'm receiving, the loved one will revise it in one or more ways so that I can understand it. I've also found many on the other side have a sense of humor. At the end of the session, I'll ask my client if they have any other questions. On a rare occasion, a client will say they wished that a certain loved one had come through. I'll ask them to invite that loved one in silently, so I don't know who it is. I've had great success with this method, but it's not guaranteed. In fact, I can't guarantee who'll come in for your reading. That's up to your loved ones. To this day, I am still in awe of every reading and how each loved one chooses to come through and how they tell their story. The healing that happens on both sides is incredible. I truly feel so honored and humbled that people let me in to be a part of this journey in their lives.

Sometimes a client forgets to ask a burning question during our session, which is why I'm happy to answer *one* question by text after the reading. Also, if I feel a client needs it, I'll offer long distance energy work after a session at no extra charge. I believe part of my life's mission is to be as supportive and helpful to my clients as possible. That's why I don't charge for this added service.

My goal with every reading is to help each client find closure and to move forward in life, especially after hearing repeated validations that their loved ones on the other side are watching over them. I also want my clients to feel a release of energy and to feel lighter when the reading is over. I've had clients tell me that they felt as if a weight had been lifted. Others have said their nagging back pain had vanished after the reading. It's hard to move forward if they're carrying emotional baggage from someone who has passed. Sometimes connecting with that person allows my clients to stop feeling stuck.

I love connecting everyone with their loved ones. I always feel so honored to pass their messages to my clients. Every reading is different; yet every reading is filled with purpose and love. I'm so thankful for what I do every day!

Seven Steps to Prepare for a Reading

Clients often ask what the best way is to prepare for a reading. There are several things people can do before a reading to improve the quality of the information coming through. A reading is an exchange of energy, and the client is a big part of that energy exchange. Below are six steps to maximize the success of a reading.

1. Meditate before a reading to ground yourself and allow yourself to be more receptive. To support you in this effort, I've created a relaxation meditation for readers of this book! Visit **https://www.MariaVerdeschi.com/gift** to claim it.

2. If you don't meditate, then go for a walk around your neighborhood. Being outside will ground you so your thought processes will be more focused.

3. Make a list of questions. Most of the time, questions are answered before the list is pulled out, but it's good to make a list, so you don't forget anything.

4. Invite whomever you want on the other side to come through to give you a message or obtain closure. Do this in your mind—no talking required!

5. Come to the reading with an open mind. Generally, what comes through is always for the highest good of all.

6. Be sure you're truly open to having a reading. Feeling pushed into a reading is never good. I've had clients closed off because they felt pushed into a reading. All I see

then is a curtain closing. When the curtain is closing, I feel like I am violating my client's energy by going any further. I always stop when this happens, although it's only happened three times in the thousands of readings I've done. I'll ask my client if they want me to continue, and I will abide by whatever their decision is.

7. During the reading, sit back and enjoy all the messages from your loved ones. They often have a great sense of humor and enjoy making you laugh. There's no need to be afraid. You can record the reading and listen to it again later. My clients always hear important information by listening to the recording that they missed during the live session.

Losing My Parents

Saying goodbye to anyone you love is hard. I believe losing your parents may be the hardest loss; at least it was for me. My parents passed under different circumstances. My mother died first in 2009. My father lived another seven years before finally leaving this earthly plane. While I am a medium, in the case of their passing, I was also a daughter. I was managing my emotions while also feeling theirs. It was hard, especially losing my mother to whom I was close. In part to honor them, I'm sharing their stories here.

Mom

For a year and a half, my mother had been battling non-Hodgkin's lymphoma. I was under the impression she was in remission mainly because that's what she'd told me. In May 2009, while at my daughter's soccer practice in chilly Michigan, I talked with my mother's nurse in Florida where she and my dad had moved.

The nurse was vague about the seriousness of my mother's illness. When I asked if I needed to get on a plane tomorrow, she answered, "Yes." Her response surprised me because I thought Mom was just sick. Mom had assured me that she'd beaten her cancer, so I had no thought about it returning. I mean, why would my mom lie to me about that?

I flew to Florida the next day. When I arrived at the hospital, I immediately went to the nurse's station. They called the doctor and, within five minutes, I learned Mom's cancer had returned and that she had about ten days to live. I asked if my parents knew because this message clearly was lost as it never found its way to me. The doctor assured me they both knew and were in complete denial over the news. Who can blame them? My mom had been through so much in the past year and a half. She had many rounds of chemotherapy and a stem cell transplant that past October. That surgery took so much out of her. She set a goal of being back in her condo to watch the Macy's Thanksgiving Day Parade, and she made that goal! I was beyond happy for her. I talked to her on the phone during the parade. I felt so grateful that she was home and happy. But the next February, she became ill again and was readmitted to the hospital. This time it wasn't cancer, for she was cancer free. The doctor told me so. So, sometime between March and May, her cancer returned. This time she wasn't going to win.

With this shocking news still ringing in my ears, I went to see my mom. She was so happy to see me, and I had to act like nothing was wrong. I could feel the energy of death surrounding her, but her doctor told me not to talk about her dying, so I didn't. I talked about everything else including when she'd be going home. I had already told the doctor that she wouldn't be dying at the hospital. My parents lived in a beautiful condo on the fifth floor overlooking the ocean in Florida. It had always been their dream to retire in a place like this. I knew it was my duty to get her back to her beautiful condo so she could lie in her bedroom where she'd be comfortable and surrounded by her beloved collection of nearly one hundred dolls.

Before leaving the hospital, Mom was visited by the hospice nurse. My mother was terrified. Her eyes were opened wide and full of fear and pain. I immediately told her everything would be okay, that hospice needed to talk with her so we could take her home. I told her she was going to be safe. Everything I told her was true. I didn't lie about a thing. She was going to be okay and safe, just not in a way she wanted. My mom's fear of dying was so intense. The energy surrounding her was painful and heartbreaking.

The next day we took my mom home. As we got her settled in her bed, I glanced at the sliding glass doors that led to the balcony off my parents' bedroom. I remembered all the times I'd spent sitting on that balcony overlooking the ocean with my mother. We'd had some great conversations while listening to talk radio. Now she was too weak to sit on the balcony, but she was so happy to be home.

My father was still in complete denial even though the nurses and doctor, speaking to him outside of Mom's hospital room, had been honest about her prognosis. I knew my mom needed hospice care so that the nurses would take care of all the things Mom wouldn't want me doing. My mom was a private person, and there was no way in hell she wanted me changing her.

It took my dad until the next morning to figure out we needed help. Hospice started, and I was grateful for the peace of mind their presence gave my mom. I oversaw her numerous medications. I made a chart and checked off the pills and the times as each was given. I made sure she was comfortable and getting everything she needed. I made her anything she wanted to eat. Sometimes she'd maybe take a bite or just smell it. I didn't care. The important thing was she knew how loved she was and that she felt safe.

My mother and I were extremely close. I knew she was afraid of leaving this life. I also knew that it would be much harder to leave with me sitting next to her. I knew in my heart that my presence would hinder her process and that I was going to have a hard time letting her go. As painful as the decision was for me, I knew I needed to leave. I needed to put her needs first and set aside my aching heart and sadness. After making sure my mom had everything she needed and making sure all of the hospice people were a good match (I fired one and asked that my mom's two favorites be the only ones with her), I flew home to check on my girls.

I arranged for a few people to visit her in the two days I'd be gone. I told Mom I'd be back Friday, and she was good with that. Her sister and niece came to visit one day. The next day, her friends Marcia and Barry, the maid of honor and best man in my parents' wedding, came to visit. Marcia later shared that my mom told her she was afraid of dying and had asked Marcia if she would be okay. Marcia reassured her and reminded my mom that her father would be waiting for her, which cheered my mom. Her father, Felix, was my mother's favorite person on the planet. Her father died suddenly of a heart attack about a month before my parents' wedding. I don't think my mother ever fully recovered from her father's passing.

After Marcia and Barry left that night, my mom stopped talking. The next day was Friday. During a call with my dad, I asked him to put the phone to her ear so I could tell her I'd be with her in a few hours. She passed thirty minutes later. For me, this confirmed she didn't want me there when she passed.

After I arrived later that day, I went into robot mode. I had to take care of my father and help him with the arrangements, which, oddly, included boxing up my mother's doll collection. While I was going through the motions of making arrangements, I would ask her to make sure I was picking the correct things such as her outfit, how her makeup should be done, and most importantly what her eyebrows should look like. She was picky about her eyebrows! I was going to honor everything she needed that day right down to the sparkly nail polish and the jewelry she was buried with, including her Betty Boop watch. My mom loved Betty Boop! I made sure everything was perfect for her—just the way she would have wanted it.

Even though I'm around spirits and other people's loved ones all the time, it's quite different when it's someone I love. When it was time for the viewing at the funeral home, I almost passed out and threw up. I finally broke down sobbing. I couldn't move, so my father dragged me up to her casket. Never drag anyone up to a casket if they don't want to go. I paused and looked at her for a second and then left. I heard her voice, and this made me sob harder. I already missed her like crazy, and now I'm hearing her at the funeral.

Because my parents were originally from New York, my mom had two funerals, one in Florida and one in New York. Her family has a mausoleum in Calvary Cemetery. She's buried with her father just where she wanted to be. I'm positive she loved having two funerals; she loved being fussed over. I honored my mother through the entire death process, and it was my duty to make sure things were done just the way I knew she would want them done. I believe in my heart and soul that I did everything she wanted.

Dad

My father passed away in August of 2016. I remember hearing the news on a Friday while my daughter and I were going through records at an estate sale. He'd hit his head on Thursday while on vacation in Germany and wasn't expected to live past Sunday.

I already knew he wasn't ready to cross over and would linger for about a week. I called the hospital in Germany, where he was in the ICU. I couldn't get anyone to put a phone up to his ear so I could tell him I loved him. It was extremely frustrating! I debated about flying to Germany but decided not to because it would have strained my budget. I knew Dad would understand.

By Saturday, he was in a coma, and I was getting messages from him. By Tuesday night, I could tell he needed help crossing over. I kept hearing him say he was afraid and asking if it would be "safe" for him to go. I assured him that he'd be safe; no one was going to hurt him. I told him that Mom, his sister, and his mom were all waiting to greet him.

As he was crossing over, I saw him at age four. That's how scared he was. It was as if he'd gone back to a time where he needed the safety of his mother. My mom was there to take his hand and escort him to the other side, where his mother and sister were waiting for him. My father was a young soul and is learning much on the other side. I was grateful to be able to help him on his journey by making it a little easier and to help him feel safe.

Chapter Three

THE DEATH PROCESS

Just as there's a process to begin life, there's a process for its end.

In our society, death is often an unwelcome visitor associated with pain, loss, bereavement, emptiness, and endings. As a topic of conversation, especially with those who are ill or elderly, death brings a feeling of finality that many people are afraid to face. The unknown, whether it's the process of death or what comes after, leaves those living and dying paralyzed.

I'm here to reassure you that death isn't the end for your loved one; they've moved on to a different kind of life. Death isn't the end; it's the beginning. Know that while you can't see them, they're nearby or can be called to you by making a simple request that they become present in your life again.

When a woman is expecting her first baby, she moves into education mode to learn everything she can about the birth process and how to manage a newborn. In addition, friends and family host baby showers where everyone plays games, presents her with gifts, eats great food, and laughs a lot. Joyful expectation is the prime emotion.

But this rarely happens at the end of life, and I think this should change. What if we had a party at the end of our life where friends and family joined in a celebration? How wonderful would it be to hear how much you're valued and loved *while you're still living*? What if it were commonplace for the dying person to decide with whom they wish to spend their final moments—and that decision is respected because everyone wants to do what's best and most supportive for their loved one? As grief begins to surface, it can be hard to do what's best for the dying person. Too often they stay in this life much longer than necessary to take care of their loved ones' emotions. Saying goodbye isn't easy. But remember, it's your loved one going through the process. You're there to make it easier for them—not the other way around.

Fear of Dying

In Chapter 2, I relayed the story of my mom's passing. She was so paralyzed with fear that even talking about death wasn't allowed. When she came home from the hospital, she was still talking about recovery. She was in denial. There would be no recovery for her; she was in her end-of-life journey. My mother's fear was palpable. The air in her condo was so thick with fear that I had to take breaks and leave.

When I was with her, I tried to make everything go smoothly and ease her fears.

It's only natural to fear the unknown. A dying loved one may be preoccupied with thoughts of "What's next? What will happen to me?" A religious person may worry about their afterlife destination—heaven or hell. They may also be afraid of leaving us behind and wonder if we'll be okay after they're gone. Looking back at their life may give them great joy or great pain. Regrets may overwhelm them. By far, the most common consideration is that this is *the end*. Death is so very final. Not knowing what the final moments may be like or how death will descend can invoke paralyzing fear. When a person dies, they recall their entire life: the good, the bad, and everything in between in an instant. I've seen it happen, and it's clear to me that we're our own judge. Once this life review is over, the person is filled with white light and a sense of peace and happiness. A sense of calm fills the room that holds their body. The brilliant white light that people speak of is the release of the cords and the movement of the soul toward its next destination. Where the soul ends up depends on the spiritual development of that soul. I have done readings where my client's loved one was still working things out on the lower astral world before ascending to a higher plane. Others go straight to what we call heaven.

If I'm assisting a person in crossing over, I will start giving the family messages immediately. The departed one wants those left behind to feel their love and connection. Sometimes they bring up memories. They might have an apology for someone, or they might bring up a situation where they feel they failed and are now taking responsibility for it. This happens because in death the ego is gone. Feelings such as shame or guilt no longer exist.

It's so beautiful to witness the newly departed soul meet the loved ones who've gone before. Those souls are there to grab their hand, to guide them, and to dismiss any fear they might be holding on to. I've seen loved ones waiting with a long-ago family pet or a beloved animal of the deceased that they've been taking care of in the spiritual realm. Between the efforts of the living and those who've already passed, fear about the transition from life to death will be dispelled. Birth and death should both be celebrated for the miracles they are.

Soul Vibrations

Not every soul goes to heaven, but I can assure you that there's no such thing as hell. Our souls travel to where the "soul vibration" allows it to go. For those with a higher vibration, this means a heaven-like place where the soul can rest and reconnect. The souls with a slower, heavier vibration have more work to do before they may ascend into that higher plane. Think of it as "soul school."

The souls that need added schooling didn't learn critical lessons while living. This can include those we consider criminals or evil people, but it can also include people who sacrificed for everyone else and never took care of themselves. Soul school is a karmic response to help the soul expand, grow, and (hopefully) not repeat past offenses.

Coma—A Death Delayed

When our loved ones are in a coma, most of the time it's because the patient is afraid of what's waiting for them in the afterlife. They may be afraid to leave their loved ones, and they're still corded to everyone and everything in the physical world. It's our job to help them move forward and cross over without fear. It's our job to make sure they have dignity and grace. It's our job to try and understand what they need to make their journey a joyful one.

I've helped many people in a coma cross over. First, I listen to what they need to let go of this world. Then I pass their messages on to loved ones with a request to follow through with whatever the person needs to move on. I consider helping coma patients the major reason for why I'm here this lifetime. It's my reason for being. Helping a loved one cross over without fear and in peace creates a healing experience for the entire family. I've worked with families that weren't close, yet the whole death experience brought them together again stronger than ever. It's one final way the dying person can contribute to their loved ones' lives.

Teri's story illustrates the importance of clear, loving communication with those who can no longer communicate for themselves.

Teri

I was introduced to Maria in 2018 by a good friend of mine. She'd told me stories about how Maria had helped her communicate with her husband who died unexpectedly a few years ago. She told me how at peace she was after her meetings with Maria.

During my first meeting with Maria, I was able to communicate with my mother, sister, and dad who passed away forty-one years, eight years, and three months ago respectively. All three of them opened a conversation with me through Maria. At the end of the reading, I was relieved to know they were all together and happy. In fact, I learned that their life in the afterlife is peaceful, the environment is nonjudgmental, and they're all in their "happy place." I'm grateful to be able to understand and accept these communications.

At the end of the meeting, Maria told me that my mother wanted me to know that my brother was extremely sick. She made sure I understood that he was terminal, that the three of them would be waiting for him, and for me to tell him not to be afraid. She told me he was being very hard on himself, that he was afraid, and that I needed to stress to him that he would be fine; there's nothing to be afraid of. My mother was also excited that she'd be able to be with him again.

My brother was diagnosed with terminal cancer in November 2017 and passed away just days shy of the first anniversary of the diagnosis. Until the day he went into a coma, he was adamant that something would change. He was convinced he was going to beat his diagnosis. The hospice nurses told us they'd never seen anyone fight dying like he did.

Before he lapsed into a coma, I had a long talk with my brother. I learned that he was afraid to die. When I asked why, all he would say was "I've done some very bad things." I told him about my visit with Maria and what our mom, dad, and sister had to say. I also told him that they'd be there waiting for him when he passed and that everything would be okay. I thought this would bring him peace, but it didn't.

On November 12, 2018, my friend who recommended Maria sent me a text asking for an update on my brother. I texted that he'd been without food and water for eight days, in a coma-like state for five days, and was still fighting death. I added that I was struggling with his decision and strength to continue to fight. Then my phone rang. It was my friend. She was with Maria and Maria needed to talk to me right away. I protested a bit as I had a meeting scheduled with Maria the next day. My friend pressed, and I finally relented by saying, "Have her call me." She said that Maria needed to meet me at my friend's house. My response was, "Are you kidding me? You're really scaring me." She said that I didn't need to be afraid and that what I would learn would bring peace to my brother, my family, and me. I got in the car and drove over.

Maria answered the door when I arrived. She looked as if she was struggling with something. She shared that my brother had "come in" to her, and he needed my help. Normally, she can tell people that come to her that this wasn't their time, but she said she couldn't get my brother to leave. It was obvious to her that he was afraid and struggling. Maria felt she needed me to help him that night.

It was my family's turn to speak. My mom, dad, and sister were excited and talking over one another. They needed me to help my brother pass peacefully because I was the only person he'd listen to. In other words, I needed to talk some sense into him. My sister told me he was in the process of crossing over, but he got scared when he saw Mom.

My job was to tell him that it was time and that my mom, dad, and sister were waiting for him. He needed my help because he was afraid that he was going to hell. He needed proof that everything was going to be all right. My family told me the proof he needed was in the Bible, and that we needed to find passages related to forgiveness. I was nervous. How could I do this given I live over two hundred miles from him?

Plus, I wasn't sure I was the one who should be chosen to do this. After all, I was a lapsed Catholic. I still believed in God, but I didn't actively practice my faith like my two sisters. Apparently, I was the only one my brother would listen to because I was the "sensible one."

I didn't know any forgiveness Bible passages, but my good friend did. She went into her office and found seven verses related to forgiveness and printed them out. She gave the pages to Maria who wrote a number from one to seven next to each verse. I was given specific instructions as to what to do.

I called my brother's wife and explained what was about to happen. She put the phone up to his ear, and I talked to him.

Using a loving, calm, and measured voice, I:

- Told him he was forgiven for all his sins; they've been wiped clean.
- Said his name and then read the seven Bible verses in the order given.
- Told him he's clean, ready to go, and that he's been forgiven. (That day the hospice nurse gave him a bath and shave).
- Reminded him that his time on earth provided him with all the lessons he needed to learn, and those lessons were complete. He changed his ways by returning to the faith. I reminded him that he'll no longer be judged.

When I finished, his wife told him that she loved him and that she would be okay. Her voice was soft, loving, and resolute. She meant what she said.

She later told me that when I was talking to him his heart rate increased significantly, and his breathing became more labored. After the call, he appeared to be more at peace, and his breathing had calmed down significantly.

My brother lasted through the night. He appeared at peace and much calmer than the previous eight nights. With his two children, ex-wife, and wife with him, my brother passed away peacefully around noon.

I kept my meeting that day with Maria. I had a lot of questions about why I was chosen to help my brother cross over. On this day, my mother, father, and sister were relaxed and speaking calmly to Maria. She told me how privileged I was to be picked to help my brother. I sure wasn't feeling that way.

The first person to come through was my brother. He spent twenty minutes telling me how happy he was, that he was out of pain, and he was at his "happy place in life." He confirmed that he could see my mom, dad, and sister. He explained that it took him a bit to fully cross over and that he couldn't have done that without my help. He was so grateful I gave him permission to let go and forgive himself. He thanked me!

I would like to say that evening I was at peace, but, honestly, I was still confused and needed time to process. It took me a couple of months to understand this really was a privilege and to be thankful I was strong enough and open to helping my brother. It was a blessing that I was chosen. I realized our passing from this life to the "afterlife" is a happy place, peaceful, and positive. There's nothing to fear with death. It's a world free of judgment and full of acceptance. I understand now how lucky I was to be the person chosen to help.

The magical red house of my childhood

A view of the house from our driveway

My father's sign that perfectly described our house

Aerial view

Clive's house

Clive and me

My parents' first date

My mom looking beautiful during college

Mom and Dad on the beach at Coney Island

Mom and Dad having fun

My parents on their wedding day

My parents on their honeymoon in the Poconos

My parents met the Heaney's on their honeymoon
and became lifelong friends

My mom in the Poconos

My mom in the yard on Long Island

My mom with her beautiful smile

My dad during his NASA days

A fun day with Dad

Mom pushing me on the swing on Long Island

First night in my big girl bed on Long Island

My birdhouse nightlight

Me at 18 months

Communicating with a cow at age three on vacation
in New Hampshire

Our family cat, Ming Toy, in New Hampshire

Our cottage in New Hampshire

Felix Verdeschi with the family dog

My mom with her father,
Felix Verdeschi

My mom at age ten with her
sister, Sharon Ann

My beloved Sammy passed
in November of 2018.
He is missed every day.

My son Michael's dog, Lola,
who passed tragically
on Christmas Day 2017

My great grandmother, Maria Verdeschi, had the family mausoleum built in the Calvary cemetery in New York

Maria Verdeschi on the left, sons John and Ralph and
her brother Paul on the far right. Early 1940s in her butcher
shop Sunnyside Queens NY

Chapter Four

CLIENT STORIES

This chapter is dedicated to several client stories to illustrate the many ways in which I work with my clients. I consider my work to be sacred, and I'm honored to be a part of the most intimate details and experiences of peoples' lives.

Many of the stories have been written by my clients. Others have given me permission to write their stories for them. While it will be obvious as you read them, I've also noted the stories I've written with an asterisk (*).

These stories are arranged in three loose categories: crossing over, messages, and signs.

Client stories have been edited for clarity and length, and some of the names have been changed to protect their privacy.

Crossing Over

Connie

My sister Joanne had a severe cat allergy. Sadly, she went into respiratory distress after being exposed to cats that put her into a coma. So severe was her reaction that she was declared brain dead but was being kept alive by machines.

Our father had been given the gift of life through organ donation when he had a liver transplant years before, adding seventeen joyful years to his life because of the kindness of the donor's family. We felt a sincere obligation to repay the gift our father received, so there was no question that Joanne's organs would be donated. So, we waited to hear if Joanne was a match for organ donations as the machines whirred and hummed.

I looped Maria in because I knew Joanne would want to talk to us. Joanne wanted to communicate with her ex-husband, Manny, and sons. Maria called while we were in the waiting room of the hospital. I put Maria on speaker phone, and Manny listened intently.

Joanne apologized to Manny for several mistakes she'd made during their marriage that were traumatic for them. These were private moments that Maria could have never known. Manny began shaking and crying as he listened. He had finally been vindicated for some of his actions and forgiven for his sins against his wife. Joanne's message ended with a joyous appreciation for Manny and wrapped up with love, kindness, and compassion for the wonderful years they shared together in their marriage.

Manny dropped to the floor crying and sobbing with his hands together in prayer, thankful for those words he'd longed to hear. In my opinion, this was a life-changing reconciliation between Joanne and Manny and a moment only Maria could have facilitated. I don't believe my sister was ever going to reconcile with Manny while she was living; the wounds on earth were too deep. I am grateful that Maria allowed me to witness this moment of reconciliation.

The news came back that Joanne was a match. The organ transplant team arrived at the hospital at 2:00 a.m. to harvest her organs. The transplant team gave us a few minutes alone with Joanne before taking her to the operating room. This was a very intense and climactic moment. It would be the last time we'd ever touch, hug, or hold our sister. Our sister Nancy knew we needed to calm down, so she turned on a Pandora music station. The song that filled the room was profound, and Nancy hadn't purposely selected it. The song? *I'm Leaving on a Jet Plane* by Peter, Paul, and Mary!

This was profound because Joanne spent fifteen years as a flight attendant and flight supervisor for Spirit Airlines. There couldn't have been a more appropriate and loving song. It wasn't a coincidence; we knew she'd selected this song to tell us how much she loved us. Nancy, Barb, Samantha, and I stood in a circle holding hands. We were all linked to Joanne—one circle of love. Then we started singing this song at the top of our lungs. The night nurses in the hallway heard us and rushed into Joanne's hospital room. They joined in, too, swaying and singing this beautiful song with us. When the song ended, they wheeled Joanne to the operating room.

The surgeons told us, as they withdrew Joanne from life support, she could die quickly, or it was possible her body could start working to keep her alive. If her body fought, she could linger as long as a day or two. If this happened, her tissues and organs would be destroyed due to insufficient nourishment. As harsh as it sounds, we needed to hope that she passed within twenty minutes of the machines' withdrawal. Maria communicated this information to Joanne. She also counseled us to talk to Joanne, tell her she's forgiven her for all her earthly misdeeds, and that it's okay to go.

I had the honor of being next to her head in the operating room and talking to her in her right ear. Her son was talking to her in her left ear. We spoke soothingly to Joanne and told her how much we loved her.

My sister was pronounced dead fifteen minutes after the withdrawal of life support. Supporting Joanne through the death process remains one of the most important events of my life. I'm forever grateful for Maria's counseling as Joanne passed to eternity.

Marlowe

Maria and I were acquainted through the years as our daughters went to school together since kindergarten. I don't think we had many conversations until our girls reached high school, and we began carpooling our girls to their new school. Maria and I quickly learned we had an awful lot in common. Not only were we both single moms, but we both also had a love and understanding of energy work and the art of healing. Maria was always picking up on energies and circumstances, often giving me food for thought (whether I wanted it or not!).

When my mother became ill and was dying from cancer, Maria was so dear to me during that time. She'd spend hours on the phone with me coaching me through the beautiful experience of helping my mother pass. It was through Maria's intuitive wisdom that I was able to know what my mother needed in her final days.

Maria knew who my mother had unfinished business with, and she knew the words that needed to be spoken. She knew and described the guardians ready to help my mom from the other side. She knew my mom's favorite color and favorite flowers. Maria offered me so much wisdom and advice. I followed most of her suggestions, and, through Maria's advice and the gift of Reiki, I helped my mom let go of her earthly existence. It was so beautiful, peaceful, and amazing. Maria was an Earth angel brought to me!

I mentioned I listened to *most* of Maria's advice. Today, years later, I wish I'd listened to all her advice! During the time with my mother, Maria said one thing that stuck out as it was repeated a few times.

She'd tell me that something or someone *wasn't* my responsibility. At that time, I said to myself, "Of course, that's *not* my responsibility!" However, today I'm still dealing with what I *made* my responsibility, and it's been a costly lesson. Maria knew years ago that I was heading in the wrong direction. Perhaps I had to walk through the lessons myself. Had I just listened to Maria in the first place, I'd have saved myself four years of headaches and heartaches.

A couple of years after my mom passed, Maria invited me for a reading. Feeling honored, of course, I said yes! During this reading, Maria picked up on the stressful things in my life. She knew my husband was in the wrong job. She knew my brother was in some trouble. She knew my health was in distress. She knew I shouldn't move forward with the business venture I was considering. It was an amazing experience to have a reading from Maria! With every scribble of her pen, she offered more wisdom and enlightenment. Maria is a talented medium with a heart of gold. She has an amazing gift. I'm blessed to have benefited from Maria's gift! She's one in a million!

Sharon

One of the most profound experiences I've had in my life was when Maria helped my mother transition. My mother had been sick with Alzheimer's for many years. It finally came to the point that she needed to be placed into hospice care. As a family, we were relieved that she'd finally be at peace and her whole self again.

After being in hospice for a week or so, she wasn't letting go. I knew deep in my heart that something was holding her back, so I decided to call Maria for help. She was amazing. She told me exactly what was holding my mother back. My sister and I had an idea of what it was, and Maria confirmed it, despite knowing nothing about my family history. She explained to me what my mother needed to hear from both my sister and me so that she'd feel comfortable letting go.

Within two hours of talking to Maria, my sister and I both had a conversation with our mother. Once we finished, she passed away. It was one of the most peaceful and beautiful things I've ever experienced.

Shortly after my mother passed, Maria did a reading for my sister and me. She gave us such a sense of peace that we were able to let go of things we'd been holding on to. Maria works with a sense of love and gratitude for those passing and those left behind. I'll always have the comfort of knowing that my mother passed with no fear or regrets.

Alisa*

Alisa and I had a mutual friend, Carolyn. I contacted Carolyn early one day to ask about Alisa's grandmother as I'd been picking up on Alisa's grandmother that day. Carolyn told me Alisa was on her way to California to see her grandmother in the hospital.

I told Carolyn that I was seeing a flood where animals were being swept through a house and cars were floating. I also saw a doll. All of it was shown to me like a black and white movie. Carolyn contacted Alisa and asked if she'd like my help going through the process. She immediately agreed, and she sent me a text.

I told Alisa about what I was seeing. She was shocked. In the 1930s, her grandmother had been in a great flood in Virginia. The only thing she could grab was her doll. She said animals were caught in the water and being pushed through houses.

Alisa expressed concern because she could feel her grandma hanging on. She asked me why and if her grandma needed something. I could see that Alisa and her grandmother were close. Her grandmother was like a mom to her. I immediately felt her grandmother wouldn't leave with her still in the area. I kept getting that Alisa needed to go to the airport. While she didn't want to leave, she did. When she arrived at the airport, she called her brother and asked him to tell her grandmother that she was at the airport and that she loved her. Within four minutes Alisa's grandmother passed.

Heather

When I first came to see Maria, I had an agenda. It was to figure out the mess that had become my nonexistent love life. Instead, I walked away with a profound new understanding of the importance of why I do the work I do.

I remember Maria asking me what I did for a living because she was getting a whole posse of folks who had crossed over coming in. She asked me if I worked in healthcare because who else would have this many people barging in?

I told her that I'm a nurse who works on a unit that has more than its fair share of patients passing. What happened next still floors me to this day. She asked if I'd recently experienced the deaths of three women and two men over the past few weeks. I had. While I was trying to wrap my brain around the fact that she knew this, she honed specifically in on one patient who gave her detailed information on how he'd passed as well as information on our connection and conversation. There are no words to describe the feeling that passed through me. She gave me details that were only known by the patient who had passed and me.

Julie*

Julie sent me a text message when she was with her grandmother who was in the last stages of life. Her grandma was in a coma-like state and not awake anymore. Julie asked if her grandma had any messages or anything. Julie wanted to make the process less fearful. I keyed into her grandmother and picked up that she wanted to feel her rosary in her hand. She told me where it was, and Julie found it. Shortly after putting the rosary in her hand, Julie's grandmother passed peacefully. Julie contacted me about an hour after she passed and asked how her grandmother was doing.

I told her that I saw a bird on her finger and a house with a large window overlooking a lake. I felt peaceful energy coming through. This brought Julie great comfort because she knew that those images were from her grandmother.

Messages

Connie

Maria's readings helped me understand why my husband Rick was taken so suddenly and so young at 58 years old. Rick died from a widowmaker heart attack while he was sleeping. It was a peaceful and merciful passing.

My first meeting with Maria was about a week after Rick passed in November 2016. During the reading, Rick gave me a list of property management things to take care of and business dealings to resolve. Maria never met Rick, but I was convinced that Maria was communicating with Rick with all the information she shared.

One of the first things Maria told me was to get the nest of sticks and moss collecting in a valley on the roof removed before winter's ice and snow had a chance to build up and damage to the roof. Ten days before Rick passed, he and my son Chris had flown a drone over the house. They discovered the roof valley with sticks, moss, and a nest of items collecting in that space. Rick was going to remove those items but didn't get the chance. This incident was only known by me, Chris, and my husband. Maria had no way of knowing about this needed roof repair.

Eleven days after Rick passed, our oldest son RJ was driving in Grand Rapids with two of his cousins. They were involved in a car accident. RJ called me from the side of the road. He was crying but relieved. After telling me about the accident and confirming everyone was fine, he said he knew his father was with him lessening the impact of the accident and saving all three of them from injury.

Rick wanted me to give his Jeep to RJ. When I pulled the paperwork on Rick's car, I discovered that the vehicle ID number described Rick's intention. The VIN is 1CFRJFBG###### or translated: **1 Car For RJ For Being Good.**

Ronda*

Ronda sent me a text message saying her beloved aunt was in a coma in the hospital. The doctors advised the family to get together because it was time to make some decisions. They learned that even if she did come out of the coma, she wouldn't be able to do much of anything. Her quality of life would be nonexistent. Ronda was at a loss as to what to do. She wanted to do the right thing for her aunt and make sure the right decisions would be made.

Ronda told me that part of the story and nothing else. I immediately heard, "Not yet! I didn't think it would be this soon! Wait . . . just wait! Don't do anything yet! I haven't made up my mind to stay or go!"

I sent Ronda a text of everything her aunt was saying. She was making it clear that she was still deciding to stay or go. I felt something had been recently discussed between them about how her aunt wanted things done when that time came. The way her aunt kept saying, "Don't do anything yet! Just wait!" in a firm, loud voice. I told Ronda not to do anything yet. She needed to wait.

Ronda told me that her aunt had told her she didn't want to be kept alive by a machine. Life support was out of the question. It was this declaration that was causing Ronda to struggle with this decision. Ronda told the doctors to give her aunt some time.

I kept checking in on her aunt. Over time, I was feeling it was more likely that Ronda's aunt was going to make it and be okay. I passed that message to Ronda, too. I remember being confident and having a "knowing" that everything would be okay even though the doctors believed she'd be a vegetable.

A few days later, Ronda's aunt woke up. She's completely fine as if nothing happened.

Mary*

When Mary came to me for a reading, she'd just moved back to Michigan and was getting her business started. I could see that health and career went together for her. I saw swirling energy around her work telling me she did some kind of energy work. Mary verified that she was a massage therapist who did energy work.

Mary's grandma came in first and then other members came flooding in like helpers. I felt they helped her with her energy healing like they were a team. Mary verified that they did work as a team.

Her mother and aunt came in. I told Mary they had a large cord wrapped around them. I felt the cord was there in life and in death. Then, I suddenly felt hot. Mary verified her mother and aunt were close. After their kids were grown, Mary's aunt moved in with her mom. One night, there was a house fire, and her mom tried to drag her aunt, who was on fire, out of the house. Her aunt died from her injuries. Mary's mom passed less than a year later.

I then began to feel a man come through who was waiting for his turn to talk. His death was sudden and unexpected. It was her husband. His main message for Mary was that she'd done "everything perfect" for his care. Mary later told me she'd wondered if he was okay with how she handled everything. That message meant everything to her.

While I was connected to him, I picked up on "brain" for him. I also picked up on him being happier after something happened. His energy changed, and he became more intuitive. The colors around him changed. I could see that he would've been an amazing energy healer. Mary verified that he had a brain aneurysm. Afterward, he was a happier person; the difference was incredible. They were married for thirty years, and she missed him greatly. Mary was relieved to see and feel how great he's doing on the other side. She was grateful to learn that he's still with her.

Jewel*

Jewel is someone I immediately picked up on as being intuitive and guided to people and places. She verified this and said she was guided to me. I showed up as she was googling for a psychic. I've had a few clients tell me this same story.

Jewel's grandmother began giving me information. I knew because, when information starts coming in, I always ask, "Who is giving me this?" I can feel energies switching, so I'll ask the question again so that I always know from where and from whom the information is coming. It's important to know who the source is during a reading.

Jewel's reading started off with me seeing and feeling a breakup or the ending of her relationship. I also felt my head literally spinning from all the stories and lies she'd been told. Jewel looked surprised. She said she was just talking to her girlfriend the day before and was telling her how her head is spinning from all the lies. She was already planning on breaking up and was so happy and relieved for her intuition to be confirmed.

Information about her career was also coming in. I was seeing lines going out to several areas, not just one. This vision was telling me she earns a living doing many things, and that she is multi-talented. I felt her creative side needed to come out more and expand.

Her father came through. He wanted to help with her business. I also felt tension with his energy. He was someone who argued a lot in life. I felt sadness with him in how he treated others and how he treated his wife while he was living. He said, "Tell her I'm sorry for being such an asshole." I felt bad saying that to Jewel but agreed that he was an asshole. He said he was doing the work on the other side to atone for the damage he did here.

Jewel was so happy to receive the messages from her father. It brought her some peace in knowing he is working on things, but it also brought her peace that he acknowledged the things he did and the way he acted while he was alive. He acknowledged his poor behavior and took ownership of it. That helped her to move forward with peace.

Jewel also had a high school friend who showed up at the end of the reading to say "hi" and let her know he was okay. I picked up about something around the head. My head started to hurt, but I wasn't one hundred percent sure why. Then it clicked. People who are shot in the head won't show me, and she confirmed this was how he passed. She felt some peace knowing he was okay.

Pam*

Pam's mom was coming in before the reading started. Our loved ones get so excited when they get to talk to us. Sometimes loved ones start hanging out with me the night before or first thing in the morning before a reading.

Pam's mom is a strong energy on the other side. She came through loud and clear. I picked up on her father, too. I was also sensing the mother was remarried, but I was feeling "off balance" between the two men. What I was feeling was that she wasn't married long to the second husband. Pam validated that the second husband was more of a companion and a friend to her mom and that they weren't married long.

When I was picking up on Pam's dad, my chest, heart, and lungs began to hurt painfully. It became hard to breathe. I asked Pam about her father's death. She said he was in a horrible car accident that crushed his lungs. The death certificate also stated he'd had a heart attack, but she said he died due to the car accident.

Pam wanted to know if her mom had anything to say about her passing. I immediately felt a lot of pain extending down my back. She showed me prescription bottles and her back where she'd had surgery. I felt that Pam's mom's passing was linked to everything she was showing me. Pam's mom told me she didn't have a good feeling about the surgery. I began to feel her fear and anxiety around it. She went forward with the surgery because she was in so much pain. She wanted Pam to know that she couldn't go on living like that, so she had to take the chance with surgery even knowing the risks involved. Pam corroborated that her mom had complications from back surgery. She added that two of her mom's siblings had died as a result of surgery. I was happy to share with Pam that her mom was doing well and that her energy is strong.

Pam's mom began to focus on Pam's and her husband's health. She kept bringing up bloodwork and cholesterol for Pam, showing me a line linking it with family health. Pam was scheduled for bloodwork soon. She acknowledged that her mom had been on cholesterol medication and has a sister who takes medication for it. Pam's mom also brought up her husband's health. She kept repeating "sugar" and saying he needed to pull his health together. She kept repeating he makes really bad food choices . . . really bad . . . and lots of sugar. She wanted Pam to know that he was on the path to becoming a diabetic. Pam confirmed everything that her mom told me. She said her husband loves sugar, gravy, and fried foods.

Two weeks after her reading, Pam's husband decided to go on a strict diet. No sweets, no late-night eating, cutting his portion size down, and eating fruits and vegetables were his new way of eating. Within three months he lost thirty pounds. He didn't do this because Pam told him what her mom had said—she hadn't told him. I believe Pam's mom was helping him start and stick to a new way of eating so that he'd have many years more with his family.

Tony*

Tony's parents came through in his reading. Tony's mother immediately brought up his sister with the boy and girl and how her husband isn't there for his family. She insisted this sister needed the family's help; the family needed to step in. After the reading, Tony told me how, just the other day, the family was talking about an intervention for this sister. His mother was validating what needed to happen.

His mother talked about the health of one of his sons. They needed to get his health in order. Tony validated he was at the doctor with him recently.

His dad also brought up "feet" and was laughing. Tony also started laughing. They used to put toothpicks in between his dad's toes while he was sleeping.

Tony asked about his new business, and I kept picking up on boundaries and a checklist. He said he was just working on the checklist. I kept hearing his dad saying it will do well, and it has done well.

Tony's girlfriend had originally scheduled the reading with me because of a recurring dream he was having. His parents were standing across the street and beckoning him to come to them. His mother was crying, "Forty-nine is too young!" He was turning forty-nine that month and was worried sick he was going to die. His girlfriend wanted to put those fears to rest. When I keyed into the situation, all I kept getting was for him to clean up his act and get healthy. I did not see him dying any time soon, definitely not at age forty-nine!

Tony admitted during the reading that he'd been paying a "psychic" for monthly "protection" for over seventeen years. He recounted how, when he couldn't pay for a few months, the psychic called him and said her "superiors" told her that she had to take the protection away. Tony was terrified. It was a threat to his children as well as himself. He made arrangements so he could continue to pay.

To say I was outraged that another living human being could bring so much pain and fear to another is an understatement. Let alone it was a psychic! He went to that person for help, and all he received was fear and a smaller bank account—for years. *Not* all psychics have your best interests at heart. If someone asks you to pay monthly for protection—*run!* You never need to pay a psychic for protection. Your loved ones protect you. I was firm with Tony. I told him to stop the payments because she had no power to cause him or his family any harm. In fact, I picked up that her psychic abilities were gone. This shows that if we abuse our abilities, they're taken away. I suggested that, with all the extra money, he and his girlfriend should go on vacation!

Tony did stop paying her and is comfortable knowing she doesn't have any power to harm him or his children.

Michelle*

Michelle's grandma came in and started talking about Michelle's sister's wedding. She talked about a conflict that involved the new husband. She used the word "cheater." Michelle's sister found out after the wedding that he did cheat. Grandma was confirming it and said they might not work it out.

The grandma also brought up Michelle's boyfriend and said, "You can't put your finger on it." She was talking about his integrity and actions. Michelle confirmed that grandma was right. Grandma was not happy with him.

But I could see a link between Michelle's boyfriend and his stepdad that was more like a father-son connection. His stepdad killed himself, and, in the afterlife, was so sorry about the way he left. Michelle's boyfriend was—and still is—deeply affected by his stepdad's death.

During Michelle's reading, a dog come through that was linked to her father. I saw a horse. She confirmed her father used to live next to a horse farm.

Then I saw a large pig. At first, Michelle didn't know what that was. I kept saying, "This pig is really large and so grateful for all of your love and help." She started laughing and said, "Yes, I remember! Years ago, I helped a large female pig with her babies!"

Then Michelle's dog came through. I kept picking up on the furry tail. The dog was small, which is how she knew it was her Peanut that she'd lost the week before. I felt the dog's death was accidental. There were complications during surgery. I told her that her dog was happy and around her now. I was also able to tell her that her grandma was taking care of her beloved dog. Knowing grandma was taking care of her precious dog lifted so much pain and guilt.

Connie

In July 2016, after my sister Joanne died, Maria did a reading for me. She told me many things about my sister's passing that were helpful for me. I felt I understand why Joanne had to leave this earth at the young age of fifty-five.

Joanne and I were inseparable growing up. In a family of nine children, we bonded tightly as we shared a bedroom for twenty-one years. We knew each other's secrets, loves, insecurities, and precious, joyful moments.

During this reading with Maria, Joanne told m that I would have a severe and dangerous he incident. Maria saw the skull and crossbon she also told me not to be alarmed because Joanne said everything would work out okay. She emphasized that the incident would be life-threatening, but I was going to be fine.

Joanne said I needed to take care of my health. I immediately went to the doctor and was diagnosed with slightly elevated blood pressure. I started on a low-dose blood pressure medication. Four months later, my husband died suddenly and unexpectedly. Then, I suffered a heart attack, also known as broken heart syndrome. Seven hours after the EMS crew took my husband out of our house to the morgue, the same EMS team came to treat me for my broken heart syndrome. As we raced to the hospital in the ambulance, two wheels fell off.

A second ambulance was called. While waiting for the second ambulance to arrive, I remembered that Joanne told me I'd have a severe health incident, but that I was going to recover and be fine. Those words gave me a tremendous amount of courage and confidence that everything would turn out okay.

I'm one hundred percent certain that I'm alive today because of the message I received from Joanne telling me everything would be fine. When I arrived at the hospital, I told the cardiac surgeon that everything was going to be fine. When he examined me, I saw that my chest was purple and black from my breasts to my chin because of poor circulation and my broken heart syndrome. The emergency room physician told my sister and son that this was an urgent and serious condition. He was worried I wouldn't survive. I didn't give up; I didn't let go. I was committed and driven to push through this incident. I owe my survival to Joanne and Maria!

Dot

Since I had experienced an accurate reading from Maria in the summer of 2017, I booked a second appointment in 2019. I needed some answers about my life. During my first reading with Maria, my mother had relayed good advice and wisdom for me. I wasn't sure what would happen during the second reading.

My main concern was my health. Since retiring from full-time work in January of 2019, I'd become lethargic and depressed. I was drinking alcohol every day. Routine tasks were put aside, and I slept a lot. I gave Maria no information at all. In fact, she reminded me to "just answer yes or no. Please don't give me details on anything."

My mother came in first. She instructed me to stop "slacking off" and told me I needed to get healthy. She reminded me of the family history of alcoholism and to pay attention to that regarding my health. She told me I needed to stop drinking, or I'd end up with a fate worse than death: confinement to a hospital bed, which wouldn't suit me at all. She told me the person I needed assistance from would come forward. Perhaps it would be a life coach or motivational person whose high energy would match mine.

Maria's throat was tight, which she said represented harsh words. In my case, it was harsh words I spoke to a close friend while under the influence of alcohol. Those words were spoken in an altered state of emotions. Maria was spot-on with this. She also told me this really bummed me out, which it did. The person I hurt thinks very highly of me. I lashed out on a matter that was none of my business. Maria's words pulled my heart. She also told me this friend was a block for me. This person loves me but blocks aspects of our relationship. She also said this person drinks a lot. As she focused, she saw the person's liver is becoming damaged.

Maria also spoke of me under the influence of alcohol and said that I was making bad decisions as a result. This behavior was not suiting me well at all, my mother related. The alcohol use was bringing my vibration down to a low level, and there were others involved in my alcohol abuse as well. Again, Maria was spot-on in bringing this forward. I was told I needed to do what was best for me.

Maria mentioned that I have true friends who are close to me and who are like family. This is true. Maria said when I made the necessary changes that I would need to share with my friends. My true friends would understand my changes. She also said some of my friends wouldn't be accepting of the changes I needed to make and that I needed to stand up for myself.

Alcohol was hindering my life and causing me to make bad choices, which is not the way I wanted to live in my retirement years. Maria told me that one couple wouldn't understand my need to change and would even try to hinder my changes. She also said it would be hard for me to let them go.

Maria, as she was being shown large Roman pillars, told me I needed to consider the true friends as pillars who would support me. My mother added that true friends are pillars, not hindrances. When I'm surrounded by true friends with higher vibrations, I'd be moving forward and at my own higher vibration. Maria noted that there are lots of pillars surrounding me in my circle. What I believe will be hard (telling my friends about my changes) will not be as hard as I think; the pillars will support me. The pillars will keep me safe, and I need to remember that. My mother told Maria that I need the pillars in my life to help me with the resistance. I need to give myself permission to lean on the pillars, and I will become a pillar and need to be stronger. Maria was hearing and feeling that I have a hard time asking others for help because I think I'm being a pain in the ass. My mom said, "Asking for help doesn't weaken you."

Maria was being shown a road lined with potholes that were deep enough to stand in with half my body. She was being told things have been hard for me to get out of, and I have trouble getting out of these things. Making changes will be the first step toward filling these holes. She went back to the close friend I'd spoken harshly to. She said the close friend can be sneaky at times with the truth, which is something I suspected. She also said I walk on eggshells around this friend, which I do. This relationship is not serving my highest good, and their vibrations are making my potholes deeper.

My mother told Maria that I needed to make a major decision about this relationship, and there would be much resistance to overcome. Maria saw a car trying to push through an immovable brick wall. She said I need to go around this wall to make it easier. Making these changes will be hard, yet they'll be easier once I start making changes and that I will say to myself, "Why didn't I do this before?"

My mother also said I needed to get outside more and breathe. She wasn't happy with me sitting inside all day. Maria then asked if I had a dog. She was picking up on it being a comfort, helping me emotionally. She felt the dog has healing energy like that of a therapy dog. I had just adopted a rescue dog from a friend who couldn't keep her. This dog definitely was my healing energy dog!

Maria had said earlier in the reading that my mom was saying the changes were to begin today. Then Maria asked when I'd be seeing the friends I needed to announce the changes to. I told her I'd see them at 7:00 p.m. that night. Maria was so happy that she offered to do energy work on me to help.

I did see the friends that evening and spoke at length with them, gaining their support for the changes. The very next evening I saw two friends. It went well with one but not the other as predicted. The one who didn't accept my changes is someone who had invited me to their home earlier that week. I declined the invitation. This person confronted me about it, and I told them why I didn't accept it. They got mad at me and left.

I truly feel that I would have remained in a bad place if I hadn't reached out to Maria for a reading. I am forever grateful for her help. Maria is a wonderful, loving, caring lady who has helped me twice with her true and heartfelt readings.

Patti O.

Despite trying to move forward, I was at a place of disillusionment and felt like I had run out of motivation and hope. I'd been through two divorces, two bankruptcies, and an eviction. I had to start over from scratch. At fifty, my life had changed drastically. I was in college, living in a dorm so that I could get a degree and a good job. I had a long-standing passion for organ donation and had volunteered with an organization for many years. When I finally graduated, I was unable to get a job there. I took a job working with eye donation instead. I intended for it to be short-term, but, after four years and several interviews, I still hadn't moved on to what I really wanted to do.

I have enjoyed having readings from several types of psychics for most of my adult life. I always asked to be shown something I'm not able to see any other way, and I always came away with something of value. A friend gave me Maria's name and said she was really gifted. I was hesitant at first because I had never had a reading with a medium. I didn't feel particularly compelled to talk to anyone on the other side, even though I had a sister to whom I was close who committed suicide years ago and a mother who'd just died. I was looking for something to feel hope again. It was February, and a blizzard made the three-hour drive impossible. I'd never had a phone reading before, but I was sure it wouldn't be as good as one done in person. I was tired, and my expectations were low.

I really wanted a message about what to do at this point in my life—something outside of my paradigm. For four years, I'd been working so hard at my job, but it was exhausting and difficult. I had to call people during the night within a couple of hours of losing their loved one to ask about eye donation. Although I believed in the mission, having to call instead of asking in person, especially during the night, was for me exhausting emotionally and physically. After talking with thousands of grieving people, I wondered how much what I was doing really mattered.

I was finally hired into the organ donation organization but not in the position I wanted. The one I had was more administrative, and I was struggling with it even after having been there about a year. I was ready to give up my dream of working with families and just find some easy job.

Maria said, "They keep showing me something I don't understand, but they won't stop, so it's important. There are many people in front of you and behind you—a large group. The ones behind you have died, and the ones in front of you are their families and friends. Your mother and sister are here but chose to step back because this message is important for you to hear at this time."

At first, I was just as confused as she was with no idea what that could mean. Then she told me that the ones who died are holding hearts in their hands and saying how grateful they are to you for helping their loved ones at the time of their death. Maria said the crowd kept growing and the emotions were gratitude and love. I knew right then what this meant. I prepared before every call I made to ask about eye donation. I focused on the family member and their loved one, silently speaking to the person who died as I tried to comfort their family member. I immediately felt chills throughout my body and a very deep *knowing*. Even though this work was extremely hard, I always felt that it mattered a great deal. This message was personal, for me alone. My brain couldn't process it in the beginning because I had an image of what I thought this reading would be. This was so much more than that. Maria then said that they want to help with my son, who had been suffering for a long time with opioid addiction. What?!

First of all, Maria didn't know what my job was let alone about my son. When she said my mother and sister were there but staying back because they wanted me to hear the bigger message, she didn't know about them either. My brain was trying to catch up with my thoughts. When it finally did, I experienced a shift in perception and understanding that has remained to this day and caused a profound expansion of my spiritual life. I never felt so deeply loved in my entire life.

From that day on, I have never doubted my path or wondered about making a difference. I got the job I wanted, and I am doing very well in my role. My life isn't perfect, but I feel an alignment that is extraordinary and deeply meaningful. That first reading was my validation and connection to a guidance/presence that I now experience often in my daily life. That message was so direct, so personal, and so intimate. I felt deeply cared for and had the sense that I will always be cared for.

JoJo*

I was honored to be invited to the funeral service of my friend's sister. After the service, I kept getting messages to pass on to her sons. I asked my friend if we should wait. She said he needed to hear his mom's messages now. JoJo's oldest son and his best friend were responsive to hearing the messages. I made sure to tell him we could do it at another time, but he was ready and wanted to hear them right away. His friend was by his side to support him through the process.

JoJo's first words to her son were about how sorry she was for actions she'd done in the past year and a half. She was so sorry for provoking him into fights every day. She was so sorry for how she left this life and the condition she was in mentally. She told him how much she loved him and his brother. She told him she wanted a better life for him. JoJo wanted her son to know her anger and passing weren't his. JoJo also brought up how both boys needed to get new friends because the boys they were hanging out with were lazy, drank too much, and were just plain trouble.

As I was giving the messages, her son and his friend had tears flowing down their faces. The messages were hitting home. Also, I noticed that both boys lightened. I felt some pressure had been taken off their backs. Both boys verified everything JoJo was saying with more tears. The emotions both boys were finally able to express and release were so needed. JoJo's son was hanging on to so much baggage and so much hate and anger. He was finally able to start a process of being released so healing could begin. He confirmed he and his mom had been fighting every day for the past year and a half. He felt it was his fault even though she was provoking him. He felt everything was his fault. He knew he was spiraling downward. He also confirmed that they needed new friends.

JoJo told both boys to step out of their fear and step into a new life. At that, both boys lost it and really started sobbing. They knew they needed to take action now before it was too late. I asked JoJo for an example concerning the boy's life. She responded, "If you move forward and step out of your fear, you can have the house with the white picket fence. If you choose to do nothing, stay where you are, and sit in your fear, you'll have a house like the way mine looked for the last year."

Her son's mouth dropped open. He said that potential was one of his fears. JoJo told her son the choices she'd made and the things she'd done weren't for him to follow.

After getting the messages from JoJo, both boys had a bright light around them. JoJo's son looked so much lighter he didn't look mad; he looked happy. He verified how angry he'd been the last month and was making a lot of poor choices. The reading helped both boys move forward and make some positive choices.

JoJo's oldest son today is doing great and really changed his life after hearing his mom's messages. He dropped friends that no longer served his highest good. He cleaned up his act. Her messages changed his life and put him on a path that will be much easier than where he was going before.

Jody

My family never discussed death or afterlife. My belief was pretty much that everything ends when we die. As I aged, I started to believe in reincarnation. I remember telling my parents that they better learn to get along and stop arguing because, if they didn't, they were going to keep coming back together until they got it right.

I was introduced to Maria in an online neighborhood website because we were both looking for a workout partner. We first met at the gym, and that's when I learned she's a psychic medium. I didn't have any experience with psychic mediums, nor did I believe in them. When we were leaving the gym, I joked with Maria that because she was a psychic, she knew in advance that we would get along. That's when she told me that my mother was in transition. I was stunned. We knew my ninety-year-old mother was suffering from congestive heart failure, and that it was just a matter of time before she passed. But I was still surprised by Maria's comment.

Because of mental illness within my family, I didn't have a great relationship with my mother. Maria told me how she had helped other people cross over, and it made me think about what I would say to my mother near the end of her days. When the time did come, I knew intuitively what to say to help bring my mother comfort.

At my first reading with Maria after my mother had passed, her spirit was present but didn't communicate much with me. Maria told me things which validated that my loved ones were indeed communicating with me, but I didn't hear anything that would end my skepticism. I didn't hear anything that blew me away, unlike how I'd been affected by seeing the impacts on others during readings I'd watched on television.

During our second reading, Maria did indeed blow me away. I can now say, without a doubt, life continues after our death, but in a different way. She began the session with a confused look on her face, saying that my loved ones were telling her about someone named Stella, like the character from the play *A Street Car Named Desire*. Throughout my life, my parents called each other Stella and Stan after the characters in the play. That was the signal I was waiting for!

Also, during the reading my cat crawled into my lap and rested her head on my shoulder. She doesn't normally let me hold her like that, but my beloved first cat that had passed away was always on my shoulder, purring away like a little motor.

My mother communicated more during the second reading. She took responsibility for the things she'd done to make my life more difficult than it had to be. She had an unhealthy attachment to one of my brothers and acknowledged that he was a darker version of her. When he was abusive to me, my mother would say, "That's just the way he is." Since he was caring for my mother at the end, it made it difficult for me to visit. She thought I wasn't visiting because I was punishing her for something. I explained that I wasn't doing it to her, that having to deal with my brother's abuse during and after each visit was asking too much of me. It was such a relief to hear her acknowledge and accept responsibility in our family's difficulties.

I tolerated my abusive brother's behavior for my mother's sake. After she passed, I chose to remove both of my brothers from my life. While my other brother wasn't abusive, he enabled my abusive brother. Now I was free.

At the end of the session, Maria asked if I had any questions. I asked if I was doing the right thing by not allowing either of my brothers to be present in my life. I'm much happier not having contact with either of them, but, at the same time, I feel like I'm letting my parents down. My parents told me that not having contact with my brothers now is justified because it was their issues that were the source of the problems. What a relief!

I was so happy to hear from both of my parents *and* from my first cat with whom I had such an unusually close relationship. Ever since that reading, I've been feeling a sense of peace and of truly being loved by my guides on the other side.

Signs

Ann

My friend asked me if I would like to go see a medium with her. I'm generally skeptical of this type of thing but agreed to go. What impressed me early on about Maria was that she told me not to say too much. She didn't want to mix up anything I was telling her with the messages she was receiving from the other side. I thought this made her very credible. She wasn't trying to pump me for information and then just give it back to me as evidence of a message. She didn't ask me many questions. What also added to her credibility was, during the few times where I didn't think her message resonated with me, instead of backing off or reversing her position, she'd say, "Just wait, and this will eventually make sense to you." Later, sometimes even several months later, her message would have meaning.

Since my first visit, I've met with Maria several times. She has primarily given me messages from my deceased father, mother-in-law, and grandma. The messages are usually about health, love, and careers. They are normal, day-to-day messages that make sense. Sometimes the words are comforting, and sometimes they're warnings, such as making sure your family member goes to a doctor about this specific symptom. I've passed her messages on to the related family members, and the messages have resonated with them as well.

My favorite message came through Maria from my mother-in-law, Lee. Lee was trying to assure me that it really was her. So, she told Maria to tell me that Lee was pretty, loved pink, and jewelry. She described her house in detail. This made me smile because only my beloved mother-in-law would describe herself this way. These were absolutely true attributes about her, so I knew it was really a message from Lee.

Maria told me that Lee was holding and petting a small animal, presumably a cat, in her lap. Lee was trying to make a point of showing her the animal. I told Maria that it wasn't a cat, but instead it was our five-pound toy Yorkshire terrier who often visited Lee in the nursing home in her final year. Our dog was so small that Maria couldn't imagine it was a dog in her lap, so she assumed it must have been a cat. Our dog provided great comfort to Lee when we visited her.

DM

My dad was amazing! My dad could do anything! Seriously he could. Throughout my whole life, random people would consistently tell me, "Your dad can do anything!" He grew up during the depression, and he could fix or build anything. He was a hard worker with a big heart, and he loved his family more than anything.

He died in May 2016 just short of his ninetieth birthday, which he was looking forward to celebrating with his family. He and I had become close in the last decade of his life. His body was failing him, and I had taken over his health care. He hated the fact that he could no longer work or do any of the things that he had enjoyed throughout his life.

That year Mother's Day was on May 8. My brother's birthday followed on May 10, and my sister's birthday was on May 12, two days later. Being considerate, Dad died May 11 in the middle of the night next to my mom—exactly where he wanted to be.

I was the one who found him looking so peaceful like he was glancing at someone in the doorway. I was heartbroken. He had become my "buddy." I was a mess in the days that followed. I couldn't eat, think, or sleep. Life was meaningless for me even though I have unwavering faith and knowledge that we never really die; we just drop our physical body. Days were long and excruciating. I couldn't imagine living life without my dad.

A friend suggested I get a reading from Maria. I wasn't sure about a reading; I mean what would that do? He was gone! Eventually, I did get the reading after three agonizing weeks of tears, death notices, and the legal paperwork one is forced to deal with all while you feel like a zombie. I was nervous and tried not to have any expectations about the reading.

Maria was warm and engaging right from the start. She wasted no time in bringing my dad through. She not only picked up on his personality, but she also picked up on the fact that he had a distinctive walk! I knew at that moment that she was the real deal, and she was in contact with "my" dad.

She told me in detail what had happened to him the night he took his last breath. It all made perfect sense to me with what I knew about my dad and about the evening of his death. That one fact alone gave me closure and answered the many questions I had surrounding that night. She also conveyed how his family was his whole world to him. She really got it. She told me more than once that he was strong on the other side. "His energy is strong," she kept saying.

I listened as she talked about how he was pushing different family members forward with little details that only my dad would know. It was an extraordinary experience. As I listened, I became calm. She assured me that "He's around."

I left the reading feeling centered and grounded again for the first time in what seemed like months!

Not long after my dad died, the family started finding dimes. Maria confirmed that the dimes were connected to my dad. Yes, there would be an occasional penny or quarter, but most of the time it was dimes. We all have our own collection of dimes, and one of my sisters has found thirty-six dimes to date.

It was important for the grandchildren to honor their "Papa" with a memorial service. On May 30, 2016, they gave my dad a heartfelt memorial. After the service, we all wrote messages on balloons, and we let them go up to heaven. It was a cool spring day and overcast in spots as we watched the balloons disappear.

A week or so after the memorial, my daughter called me from Florida. Her husband was transferring the photos and movies from his camera into their computer. She was all excited about a movie that her husband had taken. He thought he saw an image in the clouds as he transferred the file. He called my daughter over and asked her to look at it. She sent it to me, and I looked at it. We all thought the image in the cloud looked like my dad!

I believe the image in the cloud is amazing, and I know it's my dad. He was so clever and able while he was here, and I have no doubt that he could manifest an image in a cloud.

The family has continued to find dimes and get signs since my dad died. Some of the dimes have been found in bizarre locations too. I found one in the bottom of a big plastic bin where I keep Christmas paper and bows, but the one that was difficult for even the family to believe was the one my brother-in-law found inside a new, still in the package wine bottle opener. It was an inexpensive one where the plastic cover is stapled to the cardboard. He pulled the plastic off the cardboard, and a dime flipped on the floor. The same brother-in-law also found a dime on the ground coming out of a CVS store. He naturally thought it was a sign from my dad, so he went right back into CVS and bought a lottery ticket. He won one hundred dollars on a scratch-off!

During the past three years, I've found sixteen dimes. I also get signs. When I get a sign, the hair stands up on my arms.

So, when my brother-in-law won the money, I started thinking about all the dimes and signs. I thought, how can this be? Is the family imagining these things or just wishing that these dimes and signs are connected to my dad?

I meditated on it, and, on a Saturday evening, I asked my dad to contact Maria, so I'd know it's true. I hadn't spoken to Maria about my dad since the first reading. I recalled Maria said my dad had asked her for permission to give us signs. She'd never had anyone ask before. That's my dad—so polite. He would never bother Maria just out of the blue.

Twenty-four hours later, Maria contacted me and asked if my dad was at my house. There was my answer.

Patti

My second reading with Maria started out with her saying your dad is mentioning pearls. She said, "Pearl wasn't going away." She kept hearing the word pearl over and over. Maria asked if this made sense, and what was with the pearl my father was showing her? I told Maria I didn't know; I didn't wear pearls. She was persistent with the pearl; she said it was not going away. Then it occurred to me that I'd just found a necklace my husband had given me twenty years earlier. It had one single large pearl, and I'd started wearing it again that week after years of it sitting in a box. It was my dad's way of validating he was with me.

Carolyn

When I was younger, my mom would sign her name with a smiley face after her signature. It's been six years since my mom passed away. My youngest son is now fifteen. For the past several years, my son sees a smiley face almost every day. I never see them. He'll point them out, but I know that sign is just for him. It makes my heart warm that my mom is smiling down on him.

My father loved to bet a nickel. That was his favorite phrase. When he passed away thirteen years ago, we buried him with nine nickels in his hand to represent his nine children. I find nickels everywhere. I find them in my dryer in the lint catcher, not in the bottom of the dryer. I've found nickels at the bottom of a grocery bag. One day, as I was heading to a funeral, I asked my father for a sign that he'd be there. I bought a coffee and took my change. I looked down at what I held in my hand. I had eight nickels. I'm the eighth child. What a beautiful sign! I love that my father still loves to bet a nickel.

I went to another psychic, but he didn't give me much inspiration. The only thing I took away was that my mom was a cardinal. I didn't understand his message. I went to Maria, and she said my mom is a red bird; she's my cardinal. One day I was having a problem with a family member. A red cardinal flew in front of my windshield. She's not here, but, when I need her, she's there.

Connie's Story: her sister Joanne

Connie's Story: her sunset photo from the airplane showing the
orbs of her mom, her dad, and her sister Joanne

Connie's story:
her husband, Rick

Sharon's story: her mother's
high school graduation picture

Heather's story: her great
grandmother, Julia

Jody's story: her parents

DM's story: her father at age 21 and at age 89,
just a few months short of his 90th birthday

DM's story: her dad's face clearly in the clouds the day
of his memorial

AFTERWORD

I wouldn't be here without my clients or the gift I was born with. I'm grateful to be able to support people in their darkest hours and give them hope and inspiration.

Know that you may be receiving messages and signs from your loved ones just as my clients do. You simply need to be open to them.

If you'd like help connecting with loved ones who've passed, please feel free to connect me at **MariaVerdeschi.com**, where you can also schedule an appointment.

You can download the Relaxation Meditation I've created just for readers of this book at this link **https://www.MariaVerdeschi.com/gift.**

PRAISE FOR MARIA VERDESCHI

I've had two readings from Maria. If you're looking for someone to give you a cold reading and tell you what they think you want to hear—that they can sprinkle fairy dust and all your dreams will come true—well, don't call Maria. She is as near as I can tell to be the real deal. Knowing very little about me or my life and without asking any leading questions, Maria began to describe a group of people claiming to be my relatives, saying they had messages for me. She described them just as they had been in life (with some just as annoying as they had been face to face)! We then went on to discuss friends I knew as a young adult. She also helped me find clarity about events in my life now and insights into projects that I had been considering. Maria calls it like she sees it. She lets you know if she doesn't understand what she's seeing and describes it. I've always known what she was speaking about. Maria will do her best for you. The rest is up to you. ~ **JAD**

*   *   *

Death can be a very frightening and heavy aspect of our lives, but my experience letting go of my mom was easier having Maria's insight into how Mom was genuinely feeling. I reached out to Maria as my mom was passing over, and she was able to pick up on aspects of my mom's transition that helped start the healing journey for my siblings and me. My mom told Maria things that made so much sense—information that we needed to hear—which allowed her to pass peacefully. I felt so much love and warmth from Maria as she translated the messages from my mom. A few days after my mom's passing, Maria called me to say that my mom had a message for me. She said my mom was showing her yellow roses. There were yellow roses at her funeral, and I had received a card in the mail with yellow roses on the front as well as other symbolism related to my mom. I knew it was my mom's way of communicating that she was still here with me. I also felt she wanted me to know that Maria is someone I can turn to when I feel lost or need clarity. I encourage everyone to consult Maria. She provided so much comfort and helped me understand the journey after this life ends. I will absolutely continue working with Maria as I work through the loss of my mother. ~ **B**

*   *   *

My mother passed away in September 2015. Maria contacted my daughter one morning urging her to go to my parents' home quickly because my mother was transitioning. My mother didn't have long before she passed, but we felt it wasn't going to happen right away. The events of that day were incredible! Maria predicted, step-by-step, what was going to happen. She told us things about my mother that only a few people knew. She also told us that the transition was frightening my mother and asked us to find her rosary, which would give her great comfort. My mom passed just a few minutes after I placed the rosary in her hands. After what we experienced that day, I know Maria is the real deal. In late October 2015, I visited Maria for my first reading. Maria's insights were spot-on; I left feeling enlightened. To this day, incidents happen to remind me that Mom is around and watching over me. ~ **Diane**

*   *   *

Maria has a clear and comforting presence when doing a reading. She connected me with my grandma who gave me great advice for my business. My husband's dad also came through, and it was lovely to know that they were looking out for us and are always with us. Every time I get a reading from Maria, my sense of being connected to my loved ones who have passed gets stronger and more real. I'm so grateful for her presence in my life. ~ **Vivienne**

*   *   *

I found Maria through Facebook. I read the testimonials that people had written and decided to book an appointment. I have read with a few mediums and believe that those who die are still with us. I didn't have any particular questions in mind for my reading. I just wanted to see who might come through and what messages they'd have for me.

I immediately felt comfortable with her when we met. I learned that Maria meditates before each reading. During her mediation, she was given information that health was going to be a significant issue for me. True! I had had some past health issues, so I wasn't surprised, but this past year proved to be particularly challenging for me. She immediately described my father noting that he liked to wear plaid shirts. True! Dad always wore plaid shirts while working about the house. When I think of him, I always envision him in one of his plaid shirts.

Maria also connected with my mom and an aunt (who had recently passed). Mom gave Maria some messages about my sisters and me. My aunt gave Maria information about a foot. I knew she was talking about my grandfather's foot. He had lived with my aunt. Shortly before he died, he had to decide if he should have his foot amputated due to diabetic gangrene. He chose not to amputate and died shortly after making that decision. I walked away from my reading with an even firmer sense of knowing that physical death is not the end, which was very comforting to me. Those we love are always still with us. ~ **DB**

*   *   *

My first reading with Maria was so in-depth and focused on significant things with precise detail that were pivotal to my life. She was able to pinpoint information on the home I would buy, communication and specific challenges in a relationship as well as a new job offer—all of which were confidential. Maria discussed these issues without asking leading questions or fishing for details.

My second reading was equally as insightful and touched again directly on the key areas. Maria asks you not to give too much information, and I found that once again she was tuning into things that were otherwise very private. Some aspects that were offered in the first reading were confirmed by our second reading which made them even more impactful.

What makes a reading with Maria so unique is her compassion, her gentle way of speaking, and her ability to really tune in to those around me with kindness and incredible intuitiveness. I found myself both emotional and at peace with the passing of a loved one who came through with reminders that they were indeed with me every step of this journey. I can't say enough about these experiences with Maria. She has a rare gift. I highly encourage anyone considering connecting with Maria to take this opportunity to experience her incredible spirit. ~ **Jenn**

*   *   *

I've had quite a few readings with Maria especially during times of transition in my life. I've found her to be insightful and kind in her delivery of the communications she receives, and they're exceptionally accurate. Maria has also done a couple of group readings with my friends. It's a fun way to bond together and support each other's readings. She's a person of great integrity, easy to work with, and a pleasure to know. I highly recommend her! ~ **Maria M.**

About the Author

Maria Verdeschi has been developing her abilities as a psychic medium for over ten years. In addition, she is a Master Reiki practitioner and proficient in Pranic Healing.

Maria's compassion and genuine interest for each client provides for a relaxed, revealing, and down-to-earth reading. As a result, her clients leave with a sense of closure and healing with their departed loved ones.

Maria teaches classes in mediumship to those interested in developing their intuition along with classes on chakras, energy healing, and meditation. She offers phone and in-person readings and guidance and also performs home, business, and property cleansings with sage.

To contact the author, visit www.MariaVerdeschi.com or connect on Facebook or Instagram.

Made in the USA
Monee, IL
14 September 2020